Play by Any Other Name

Embracing The Play Principles
Beyond the Early Years

Michelle Simpson

For Cillian, who taught me just how much you can learn when you play.

And Darren, who supports me and my new ideas unconditionally!

For more information about my Upper Stages journey and how I implement contextual learning opportunities for my whole class, find me on Instagram @mrs_S_learns.

Foreword

A few years ago, I would have scoffed at the notion of Play in the upper stages. Isn't play for younger children? They won't learn anything; they'll just choose to play rather than learn. How on earth would I find the time for that?!

Now, however, following an enforced lockdown, teaching a class from my spare room and some research into alternative teaching and learning styles and practices, I have a new perspective. Play is a concept, an approach to learning that, if used effectively, can benefit learners of all ages. Even older pupils don't choose to play rather than learn; they learn as they play.

This book is an account of my journey into Play in the Upper Stages and how I have learned to find a balance between the traditional methods of teaching and introducing a play pedagogy to my more senior classes. It also shares some examples of how I have implemented a 'play' approach while keeping attainment and progress at the forefront of my practice.

I am a teacher in Scotland, so this has been written from a Scottish perspective, using the Curriculum for Excellence and our Primary structure. Upper Stages refers to Second Level – Primary 5 to Primary 7 – which in England or Wales would equate to Years 4-6.

Scotland	England/ Wales	
Primary 1 (P1)	Reception	4-5yrs
P2	Year 1	5-6yrs
P3	Year 2	6-7yrs
P4	Year 3	7-8yrs
P5	Year 4	8-9yrs
P6	Year 5	9-10yrs
P7	Year 6	10-11yrs

All photos are from my classroom, demonstrating resources and materials used by my upper stages class.

Chapter 1: - Why Play?

Every child has the fundamental right to play. It is in the United Nations Convention on the Rights of the Child (Article 31, if you want to check). Not only is it important for enjoyment and fun, but vital for child development. Play is generally accepted as an important aspect of development with the first eight years being cited as the most important period (UNICEF). During this time, cognitive skills, social skills, emotional wellbeing, physical motor skills and mental health are all being acquired, building the foundations for future years.

The research behind any theory or pedagogy can be cumbersome to wade through, but I will try to summarise what has been written about play already.

There is a lot out there about Play in the Early Years and no shortage of work on the benefits of play for younger children (Broadhead at al., 2010; Fleer, 2021; Palmer, 2019; Sheridan, 2011; Walsh, et al., 2010; Wood, 2013 for example). Finding research on the effects of play-related learning on older pupils is harder to find.

Play can be defined in different ways, but it is generally agreed that play is a process whose key elements are that it is freely chosen, personally directed and intrinsically motivated (Danniels and Pyle, 2018; Fleer, 2021; Gray, 2009; McKendrick, 2019b; Scottish Government, 2013). It tends to be integrated into the early years in quite an established way, but these elements can easily be considered in the learning opportunities we provide for our older learners too. We just might not call it play. We want our learners, of all ages, to be able to motivate themselves, to direct their own learning and to make good choices, don't we?

There are different types of play. Play can be creative, imaginative, exploratory, investigative, dramatic, physical, communicative and many more types aside. The skills that can be developed through play are wide and varied. There is debate over what constitutes play-based learning, whether this should include free play or play guided by teachers and in an education system where attainment results are paramount, it is difficult to imagine a pedagogy completely free from teacher involvement. Within this teacher involvement though, there is inevitably variation in the implicit or assumed knowledge about play among those teachers who may have not been formally trained in play practice or have undertaken different levels or forms of training. Differences in the way it is planned for, facilitated, recorded, evaluated, built on. Nevertheless, the essence of play-based learning is that children learn while they are at play. This play looks different for every child. Playful learning can be achieved through directed play in which it is the teacher's goal to use play so that the learner achieves pre-determined educational outcomes (purpose focused play), or it might be incidental learning, acquired through self-determined activities and exploration (free play). Ideally, we should strive to have a mixture of both.

Playful learning can enrich the learning experience of older learners, utilising the pupil-choice element of play, and giving them more responsibility for their own learning in an age and stage appropriate way (Krechevsky et al. 2019). Play can be used to increase engagement, motivation, and enjoyment through fun learning opportunities. In my support for learning roles, I have used play to great effect to engage previously disengaged learners. But can it have an impact on attainment? It has been linked with the development of language and literacy (Christie and Roskos, 2006), communication and concentration

(Danniels and Pyle, 2018) and self-regulation (Zachariou and Whitebread, 2015). These skills all contribute to progress in academic achievement and the development of these skills and attributes does not stop as learners leave the early or infant stages of their education.

The play-based curriculum was designed to bring about positive effects, not only on the immediate learning experiences of the children in the first years of primary school, but also to create positive learning foundations to sustain learning and progress in school over the longer term (McGuinness et al, 2014). Those researching the effects of learning through play tend to look at play in children up to around 8 years of age. This could be linked to Piaget's theory that the concrete operational stage begins at around 7 years of age in which children begin to problem solve, reason, and apply logic (Lefa, 2014). Free play opportunities are often made available to pupils until they reach this stage of development. I would argue, however, that the introduction of reasoning, logic and problem-solving skills is the ideal time to offer some 'play' principles to allow learners opportunities that allow them to explore these skills and apply them contextually and in a 'real life' way that is meaningful to them.

Play opportunities can be offered in a variety of ways as well. The phrase 'Continuous Provision' generally refers to having resources and areas set out in the classroom all of the time to encourage learning through play and exploration. These resources should be freely accessible to the children in the classroom during any designated 'free play' time and should stay more or less the same throughout the school year. There may also be topical or contextual areas that change from time to time to support learning about a particular theme – Fairy Tales or People Who Help Us for example. Play opportunities may be available all the time or there may be times of the day that are for play, or designated times of the week. You may have a play-based classroom or a separate room that children go to in order to play.

All nations in the UK have now developed their educational policies towards a more play-based and developmentally appropriate approach to teaching and learning in the early years. This approach is also known as an enriched curriculum and is designed to be responsive to the developmental stage of individual children. The aim of this approach was to remove the early experience of failure and promote a sense of self-competence and self-esteem. The teaching methods included more of an emphasis on play and activity-based learning rather than desk-work, in order to stimulate curiosity, creativity, social development and engagement with learning (Walsh et al, 2010).

As well as this, play is located within educational policy in Scotland through The Play Strategy, GIRFEC (Getting it Right for Every Child, the Scottish Government's commitment to providing all children, young people and their families with the support they need) and the Curriculum for Excellence (CfE, Scottish Educational curriculum, 2004). Other national organisations have also promoted play such as Play Scotland, Inspiring Scotland, The National Play Strategy for Scotland and the Smart Play Network. As mentioned earlier, my experience lies within the Scottish system, but there are also policies across the UK that support the development of Play (The Play Strategy, Play England, Play Wales, Wales: A Play Friendly Country and Play Matters).

Policy supports the provision of play opportunities for older children. This commitment to play has been further reinforced at a governmental level by moves to embed the UNCRC into Scots law (Scottish Government 2020). Additionally, the Building the Curriculum series makes specific reference to play for infant stages (Scottish Executive, 2007) and refers to play though the language of 'active learning' and 'personalisation and choice' for later years in BTC3 (Scottish Government, 2008). As mentioned previously, the principles of play are important for older learners, we just might refer to its application differently.

Play can be a powerful tool to support learning. It can be used to incite curiosity, raise engagement, and ultimately raise attainment. It can also help children make sense of what we are trying to teach them and allow them to apply it to their own world. Why should this stop after the early years? Apart from anything else, play is fun. Playful learning engages children and learning should be fun if we want children to pursue it independently and retain the information that we are teaching them.

When children play, on their own or together, they learn a whole raft of skills:

- Sharing

- Taking turns

- Solving problems

- Patience

- What they like/don't like

- Managing their emotions

- Winning/losing

- Risk taking/avoidance

- Time management

- Using their imagination

- Conflict management

- How to work with others/entertain others

- How to be alone/entertain themselves

- Fairness (and that sometimes things aren't fair!)

- Understanding scientific concepts (gravity, rotation, momentum etc.)

- Learning from mistakes

- Resilience

I could go on and on, but you get the idea.

Chapter 2: - A Short Story About Play

During the recent Coronavirus pandemic, the lockdown meant we were all put in a situation we had never been in before. In my own situation, working from home, I wanted to develop an effective method of teaching and providing opportunities for learning from a distance. Giving my learners lessons that allowed them to learn from home, with no school resources or materials, no jotters, no checking over their shoulder to see how they were getting on, and no in person support for them. The simplest solution seemed to be activities that utilised the play principles. Setting them scavenger hunts, suggesting cooking tasks, asking them to create things at home. But as the weeks went on, I began to challenge myself. Could I create play tasks that provided more of a challenge for my P5 learners?

I began looking into activities that developed skills rather than simply met attainment goals. In a measuring lesson, asking them to actually measure stuff, compare measurements and discuss their findings seemed really quite engaging. I also needed to find ways of encouraging my pupils to be more independent in their learning and take some pride and ownership of their own progress. Letting them lead their learning seemed a great way to do this. Researching something you are interested in will always be more engaging than researching something someone else has told you to learn about.

Following the effects of the coronavirus pandemic on our young people's education, professionals have been looking at alternative approaches to support our children and young people, to offset the detrimental effects to attainment (Scottish Government, 2021). Returning to school following lockdown meant organising my classroom in a different way. Initially restricting resources and then gradually reintroducing them meant I ended up with very

specific areas in my classroom, reminiscent of an early
years room with areas of play.

The following academic year, I successfully applied for the
role of Supporting Learners' Lead, tasked with supporting
the wellbeing and improving the engagement of some
targeted learners as well as aiding my colleagues in
supporting their learners. Using what I had learned during
lockdown, I took another look at the play principles –
intrinsic motivation, freely chosen and personally directed.
I spoke to and listened to my learners, found activities that
they were interested in and tailored their learning around

that. Several slime-making lessons later, I began to introduce some challenge – reading instructions, creating their own recipes, teaching younger pupils how to make slime (sorry, parents!). I even signed my targeted learners up to the Young STEM Leaders Award programme to give them some direction to their 'play' and recognition for their learning. In a nutshell, allowing the pupils to 'play' and providing learning opportunities around this raised engagement a lot. I took a lot of photos, made observations, recorded conversations, made videos and gathered feedback. I did not assess with right/wrong questions. Many of the pupils I worked with no longer require support out with the classroom environment. I believe this is because the play principles allowed them to explore their learning in a way that suited them at the time. Reports show that play could be vital in supporting children in understanding and recovering from the effects of the pandemic (Riley and Jones, 2010; Young, 2021) and this may have played a big part.

I am now back in class, bringing my play principles with me. I still teach in a fairly traditional way, but I allow opportunities for the learners to apply their learning and explore concepts and ideas in their own way as much as I can. I will explain how I do this later on. In allowing opportunities for this, I am finding that the learners appear to have a deeper understanding of the concepts they are learning about. They understand why they are learning about concepts and when they might need to use them in 'real life', which I think adds to the engagement and desire to learn more. By allowing learners to choose aspects of their learning, it gives them ownership, pride, and motivation.

So, that is how I ended up embracing a play-based approach. As you will see later on, I don't apply it all of the time and I have not abandoned more traditional teaching methods. It would be irresponsible of me in preparing learners for high school, to create a free-play environment where everything is chosen by pupils and driven by them.

What I have done, is acknowledge the potential benefits of the play principles for older learners and found a way to incorporate a playful, contextualised approach in a pedagogy that still recognises the curriculum benchmarks and attainment levels.

Chapter 3: - Play, Reimagined for the Upper Stages

Play as a tool for supporting learning is widely recognised as an effective learning pedagogy and used in the early years. The Scottish Government values play. Scotland's first national Play Strategy was published in 2013, asserting the child's right to play (Scottish Government, 2013). It stressed that **all** learning environments need opportunities for free play and that playful learning is necessary in all schools, nursery, primary, secondary, and special. Which brings us very neatly onto the subject of play in the upper stages.

Following the aforementioned pandemic, many young people needed to process the events as they impacted them, in an appropriate way. Play offers this opportunity and it also provides an opportunity to process other learning and experiences too.

The Progress Review of Scotland's Play Strategy 2021 contains recommendations that include ensuring the inclusion of all children and young people (Scottish Government, 2021). Including all children and young people, means offering the same opportunities and so perhaps play should not be an educational experience reserved solely for those in the early years. This is particularly important considering the effects of the pandemic, in which lockdown periods deprived children of opportunities to play with their friends and develop social skills and relationships. Beyond this, it continues to help learners develop their interactions with each other and build friendships and other relationships aside. Providing these opportunities in school is crucial to truly meet the needs of every child as GIRFEC demands.

Nevertheless, the benefits or impact of play for the upper stages remains widely unexplored. There is little evidence to explain why this is, but the pressure on teachers to raise attainment and produce results to show progress in learning would probably explain the lack of play opportunities provided for older learners. This seems to be changing, however, as a quick search on any social media platform for 'Play in the Upper Stages' will produce a realm of teachers bringing play into their upper stages classes. But is it enough to simply transfer 'play' experiences that work in the early years into the upper stages or is a different approach more effective?

I see many posts on social media, purportedly displaying play in the upper years. Many of these, however, show a set task, with set instructions, with an outcome envisaged by the teacher. Or a tuff tray with resources set out and a specific task set for the class. While this undoubtedly contains valuable learning for the class, it technically doesn't encompass all the principles of play unless the activity is optional – not always ideal in an upper stages class where attainment and task completion are vital! If we are considering the definition of play mentioned previously, it should be unstructured and child-led, not explicitly

24

planned by the teacher with a single, adult-guided outcome. Think of an art lesson where the learning intention is related to recognition of detail. You could model a lesson on drawing a bowl of fruit you have displayed, emphasising the shapes, proportions, shadows and then provide the class with their paper to produce 25 pictures of a bowl of fruit from different angles. Or, you could start your lesson discussing the importance of detail, emphasising shape, proportion, shadow. Then show the class a range of artwork displaying such detail but from a range of styles using a range of materials (Michaelangelo, Dali, van Gogh, and the ancient Egyptian hieroglyphs all contain a lot of detail in their artwork). Now recap the importance of the detail elements and allow your learners to create their own artwork. You will be rewarded with 25-30 very different pieces of art, and you will have allowed your learners an element of play in their learning – personal choice and, hopefully, some intrinsic motivation.

Play is essentially opportunity and experience – trying things out, exploring, investigating, and experimenting. It can offer older learners with challenge to enhance their learning if they are provided with the opportunity and materials to do so in a contextual manner. Time to measure, write, research, or create free from constraints can undoubtedly help embed learning more securely.

If we consider the previously agreed definition of play being that which includes choice, personal direction, and intrinsic motivation, this does not have to be separated into age categories or be something that children only have access to in their learning time until a certain age. If we kept the principles, opportunities, and pupil-led aspects, but gave 'play' a different name, would we as upper stages educators feel better about employing it as a pedagogy? Developmentally Appropriate Teaching? Real-Life Application of Learning? Independent Learning Experiences? Personally, I like to think of it as Contextual Learning Opportunities. In providing materials and resources the pupils have free access to, they are putting what they have learned into a context that helps them understand it, retain it and hopefully be able to apply it in real life or at least in context. Whatever you want to call it, and however it looks in your classroom, the principles remain the same. Ability levels, interests, strengths, areas for development, barriers to learning – these all differ more widely as children progress through the school as learners develop their own styles of learning and interests. As such, play can look very different from one child to the next in, for example, a P7 mainstream class.

On completion of a task, I have observed classes in which several learners regularly chose to play with the dolls and junk modelling while others chose to write a story or request to complete additional calculations from their textbook and then mark each others' work with coloured pens. All of these activities constitute play as they were freely chosen, intrinsically motivated and personally directed and appropriate to the needs of the learner. As their teacher, it was eye opening for me to see that some learners chose to continue 'learning' with textbook work. I realised that they were selecting activities that met their learning needs at that time. Since then, following a data interpretation lesson, I have seen pupils choose to survey their own classmates and create graphs, while others played Uno, or write their own short story while others listened to an audio book. It is allowing them the freedom to choose and explore their learning in their own way but also to take a break if they need to.

We do need to bear in mind though, that our upper stages classes are preparing for high school where there is likely to be little opportunity for 'play' as we generally know it. What there will be opportunity for, however, is self-driven study, self-motivation, problem-solving, working collaboratively, and independent learning. We can use our contextual learning opportunities to develop these skills and, furthermore, the play principles can be used to develop skills such as independence, patience, teamwork and encourage learners to investigate, speculate, compare, explore, problem-solve and many more. We can cultivate these skills in our young learners through play but in a way that allows them to use them in a different context as they progress through their education. It can help with their depth of understanding and recall of information, their retrieval and retention. It also provides us with opportunities for high quality assessment – assessing understanding in a new context is very different to understanding shown on a paper test.

And what if we took these principles of play – choice, motivation and drive all coming from the learner themselves – and applied them to all aspects of learning. Are we not then looking at pupil voice, contextual understanding and transference and application of skills? All vital to the raising of attainment and engagement within our schools. If we reframe the idea of play, thinking of it as more of an approach that encourages learners to be more independent, curious, and self-driven, then it becomes more palatable in the upper stages. By changing some of the ways we approach our teaching, we create an ethos of playful learning – allowing pupils an element of choice in where or how they complete their work, opportunities for pupils to elaborate on something they have learned about, variation in the amount of teacher input provided to learners – these all encourage learners to drive their own learning in their own way. Create a space where exploration and investigation are encouraged, mistakes are a comfortable part of learning, and pupils feel safe to make suggestions and ask questions.

To do this, we need to focus on what we are asking of our learners, what, specifically we want them to learn. If I am teaching my class about punctuation and need them to demonstrate their understanding and application of punctuation in their writing, does it matter if it is written in pen or pencil? Handwritten or typed? Written as a story or a comic strip? As long as the key elements of punctuation are in evidence, the other elements can be chosen by the learners. Sometimes we need to think a little bit outside the box to engage our learners. Instead of completing a writing sheet or template on setting the scene, create a scene with Lego or using Minecraft. Instead of the class watching a video of life under the sea, try going underwater with Google Expeditions. Instead of times tables flash cards, create a rap or song about the multiplication facts. Trying out different approaches encourages pupils to do the same, but it might help us find our playful side as well.

Another important element of play is that children make their activities relevant to them. Personal relevance is vital in helping learners understand new concepts and to transference and application of skills. When teaching bearings and directions, allow some exploration of the local area. Where is your house in relation to the school? Make up directions from your house to the local shop. Textbook examples are good for practise, but they don't provide a relevant link to real life. That's where we come in. I have invited pupils to write to me to persuade me into allowing something they would like for Christmas. The possibility of me acting on their writing made sure the requests were realistic, persuasive and of the best quality they could be.

Give your learners ownership of their learning, create an environment where questions are encouraged and acted on. Allow key questions from learners to lead to discussions and lessons. Allow children to drive the questioning, take charge of their own learning and they will become more autonomous in their learning, research and investigating. Hopefully contributing to the whole development of the child as a successful learner.

Chapter 4: - Barriers to Play in the Upper Stages

There is an understandable resistance to play-pedagogy and play-based learning is not universally accepted by all educators as the best tool that can meet all learners' needs. I think the word 'play' is so associated with younger learners that it is hard to conceive this approach in a P7 class preparing for the transition to high school.

There is no shortage of reasons and excuses not to try play with an upper stages class. Any teacher who has never tried it (and even some who have!) will tell you several reasons that it won't/can't/shouldn't work. These reasons are all valid:

Attainment

> We are under ongoing pressure to raise attainment, address the attainment challenge. The Scottish Attainment Challenge aims to raise the

attainment of children and young people living in deprived areas, and so those of us teaching in these areas are expected to support pupils order to close the equity gap. Nevertheless, in all areas, regardless of deprivation levels, there are still pressures to meet the needs of all learners, support where it is required and challenge where it is needed. Focus needs to be on ensuring learners are being challenged and progressing through the benchmarks. And the requirement to provide data to show these results means any change in pedagogy needs to have positive results that are robustly evidenced.

Introducing something new

The introduction of new or innovative programmes is often met with resistance. Once you have been teaching for a few years, you become accustomed to new things coming and going with a certain regularity (Class Moves or Brain Gym anyone?). It is understandable that when something new comes along, there will be some that regard it with a certain scepticism. Not to mention that the implementation of anything new will come with some kind of introductory period requiring meetings, discussions, changing resources, and who knows what else?

Time

When in the world are we supposed to fit play into our already crammed timetables? The curriculum already fills our week and with visitors, assemblies, trips, and all manner of extra things, there just isn't time to start bringing in something else.

Beyond P2 or P3, there is little time to allow pupils to simply play. The week becomes filled with literacy, numeracy and progressive lessons that will hopefully allow these learners to reach their benchmarks in a timely manner.

And when am I going to have time to set up play opportunities and tidy up after them?

Packed Curriculum

As already mentioned, our curriculum is pretty packed. If we teach Literacy and Numeracy or Maths daily, meet our target of 2 hours of quality PE and include sufficient Health and Wellbeing to make sure SHANARRI (the Scottish Government wellbeing indicators of Safe, Healthy, Achieving, Nurtured, Active, Respected, Responsible and Included) is being met, then add in Expressive Arts, RE, Technologies, Sciences, and Social Studies as well as introducing at least one additional Language are we not done?! There are over 220 experiences and outcomes to be looked at over the course of second level!

Workload

I have yet to meet a teacher whose work week sticks to the 35-hours we are contracted to. Some manage a work-life balance, many don't. Adding something else to the workload is not going to be met kindly!

With the amount of planning and marking required for working with older pupils, there is little chance of an opportunity to set up tuff trays or look up different activities that will challenge them.

All valid points. But bear with me here.

Chapter 5: - Solution-Focussed Approach

Ok, so we've come up with a whole load of reasons why Play in the Upper Stages might be an unrealistic idea. But let's look at this another way. What if contextual opportunities became part of your teaching and could raise engagement in your classroom, thereby making your teaching practice easier and/or more enjoyable? What if it could also raise attainment and independence? If you are already sold on the idea of play for the upper stages, it might help convince colleagues if you go with a solution-focussed approach. If you are not convinced yet (firstly, thank you for reading this book!), here are some things to consider:

Attainment

> If used effectively, using the play principles to create contextual learning opportunities can contribute towards raising attainment, not take

learners away from their formal learning. If current reports about the potential benefits of play for ALL children are held to be true, it can add support to their learning, which can help raise attainment, engagement, and learner wellbeing (McKendrick, 2019a). If used correctly (read: not just letting the pupils do what they want whenever they want!), opportunities for play in context can support the development of independence, problem-solving, communication, teamwork… Transferring these skills into more traditional learning activities will have a tremendous impact on our attainment levels. The increased engagement and independence are an added bonus!

Introducing something new

Henry Ford famously said, "If you always do what you've always done, you'll always get what you always got". If we never try something new, then you can't expect anything to change.

Evidence can back up your new approach, as long as it shows positive impact. Be prepared to be flexible – what works for one P6 class won't work for all classes. It might not even work for another P6 class. Chapter 7 has more information about how we can measure the impact of a play-based or contextualised approach.

If you are lucky enough to have a Senior Leadership Team (SLT) that supports your innovative approach, you will be allowed a certain amount of time to implement your change and tweak any issues – but there will need to be positive results before too long! Essentially though, it is on us as the class teacher to provide an education that meets the needs of the learners in our classroom. Research shows us that 'play' helps the brain grow and develop in ways that will benefit every area of the curriculum. It also allows

opportunity to meet the needs of several learning

styles in one go, providing its own differentiation

through the pupil-directed approach. You could be

the one bringing new and innovative changes to

the way things are taught in your school!

Time

The initial set-up might take some time, but

classroom set-up always does. If you start the

year with a Play or Contextual pedagogy in mind,

this will help your time management in the long

run. Not to mention, that older pupils are more

than able to help set up their own contextualised

areas with you in the first week of term. Once

everything is in place, make it part of your routine

for pupils to tidy things away or give certain pupils

responsibilities for organising the resources and

cleaning up after use. I have found investing in

some nice smelling washing up liquid and some cheap spray bottles has worked wonders! I have always found that there are certain times of the day that lend themselves to opportunities to play or exploration – after completing a task, just before lunch, the end of the day, Friday afternoons. It can be free play or more structured, curricular-linked play but both are valid forms. You can timetable it in or allow opportunities when it is appropriate. Whatever suits you and your class.

Packed Curriculum

Learning through Play or Context should be part of your curriculum, not an add on. I am not suggesting we try to shoehorn this into an already busy curriculum, but, instead, to offer opportunities for children of all ages access play to support their learning We already plan for Numeracy, why not make one of your lessons a contextualised numeracy or problem-solving challenge? Or have Numeracy games and activities available for those who have completed their non-negotiable task or need a short brain break?

Consider a simple game that involves a group of learners, let's say Monopoly. When played properly, during this game the following experiences and outcomes are being addressed:

HWB 2-05a	I know that friendship, caring, sharing, fairness, equality and love are important in building positive relationships. As I develop and value relationships, I care and show respect for myself and others.
HWB 2-14a	I value the opportunities I am given to make friends and be part of a group in a range of situations
MNU 2-03a	Having determined which calculations are needed, I can solve problems involving whole numbers using a range of methods, sharing my approaches and solutions with others.
MNU 2-09a	I can manage money, compare costs from different retailers, and **determine what I can afford to buy.**
MNU 2-09c	I understand the costs, benefits and risks of using bank cards to purchase goods or obtain cash and realise that budgeting is important

MNU 2-22a	I can conduct simple experiments involving chance and communicate my predictions and findings **using the vocabulary of probability**
LIT 2-02a	When I engage with others, I can respond in ways appropriate to my role, show that I value others' contributions and use these to build on thinking.
LIT 2-10a	I am developing confidence when engaging with others within and beyond my place of learning. I can communicate in a clear, expressive way and I am learning to select and organise resources independently.

Your only involvement in this activity is to source the game for them to play and give them the opportunity to do it.

Workload

The workload of a teacher seems endless. There's always planning, marking, organising, resourcing, or meetings to be done. This book is not designed to introduce something else to add to this list. On the contrary, it can provide an opportunity for a deep breath for teachers. Consider the example above – allowing your learners the opportunity to play some carefully selected board games, gives them the chance to develop skills in a relaxed way and gives you a chance to observe your class, their interactions, their application of skills. Once your play-based or contextualised, classroom is set up, offering pupils the opportunity to play and put their learning into practice, gives you the opportunity to observe them, engage them in conversation, listen to their conversations with each other and just enjoy spending time with them. I have personally found the introduction of this style of teaching into my upper stages classrooms to be invigorating and allows me to see how well a concept has been understood by my learners. A textbook page on money shows me how they understand the abstract concept, but observing them making shopping lists, browse catalogues, compare prices, calculate totals and change, and discuss whether to use their credit or debit card shows a different level of understanding that I can evidence through simple observation sheets.

These solution-focussed approaches do paint a rose-tinted view of introducing the play principles to upper stages classes. It is worth reiterating that with any teaching style, teachers need to consider what works for their learners, their setting and what works for them. There are ways to introduce elements of contextualised learning to your class without going all in. Some real-life examples of practice will be shared later in this book.

Chapter 6: - Bringing Play into Your Classroom

In my own experience, pupils do not expect to come to school to play. It is not uncommon for pupils to separate their play experiences from their learning experiences and struggle to see the connection between the two. Pupils in the upper years will probably have previous experience of school where they worked and then they got to play, or play was reserved for certain times of the day or week. The assumption that play differs from education is carried throughout the school system. As learners progress through their education, opportunities for play become less and less. Preschool activities include playgroups and playdates, breaks at primary school are known as playtime and take place in the playground. By the time they reach secondary school, playtimes and playgrounds might have been become breaks and school grounds.

It is important, therefore, to introduce the change in pedagogy to the class, involve them in the change. Explain that Playing can be a method of learning and should not be seen as separate from learning. It might help to change the terminology as explained earlier. Explain to the class that you are offering contextual learning opportunities (or call it something else that your class are comfortable with – my current class call it 'plearning' – playing and learning!). If you are new to the play principles in the upper stages or are introducing it with a view to convincing others to join you, how the pupils talk about their new approach is very important. Your colleagues, management team or parents don't want to hear pupils saying things like, "we just played today". We need to explain to them what we are learning and why we are learning through this approach.

Pedagogy

I usually start my new session with my new class talking to
them about their perceptions of learning and of play. We
then work together to discuss how we can learn through
contextualised opportunities and how we can incorporate
this into our week. I often have to revisit this agreement,
throughout the first term especially, as some pupils want to
choose the play or contextual aspects and avoid the
traditional aspects of teaching and learning. There can be
a struggle with the transition from the 'new' way back to
the 'old' way. How I explain it to my class is with the term,
'non-negotiable tasks'. These are tasks that must be
completed (or at least reasonably attempted) and that
won't go away. If not completed in the allotted time, no
free choice activities are offered, and the non-negotiable
task must be completed at another time.

As mentioned previously, in preparing our learners for their secondary education, it would be ill advised to throw out our traditional way of teaching and completely replace it with play or contextualised opportunities. By definition, play is freely chosen and intrinsically motivated and we all know pupils that would not ever choose textbook or jotter work and would not be motivated to challenge themselves to advance through the benchmarks.

For this reason, in my own practice, I still teach using Learning Intentions and Success Criteria (in line with the rest of my school) followed by a non-negotiable task, whether it be a textbook page, set number of questions, or the creation of something. Once this is completed, pupils have some choice in their follow up task. Where appropriate, I also allow some flexibility in how their non-negotiable task is completed such as seating arrangements, writing implements or partner support. I then link the available games to the learning we have been doing where possible.

An example of how this might look is:

Writing Lesson – to demonstrate an accurate use of punctuation. Differentiated through support, punctuation used and complexity of task.

Following a teaching input, the class would be set their task. I would be flexible in certain areas such as, where they sit (or stand, or lie!), who they can work with or what implements they use to complete the task –pens, pencils, or typed.

Once the non-negotiable task is completed, learners are directed towards the literacy table of activities they can access for a time such as Scrabble, Sentence Scramble, reading flash cards, free writing time or quiet reading. The activities are limited to Literacy-themed activities but are freely chosen.

Similarly, following a non-negotiable numeracy task, learners can select an activity from the Numeracy table. I regularly review these tables with the learners, ensuring there are activities that are relevant and interest them and listening to their suggestions of different resources they would like to see added.

Challenge

It is important to ensure that the 'play' opportunities provided create challenge to learners. I talk to my class about their comfort zone, where they are relaxed, and their stretch zone, where they can learn. I try to provide play opportunities that allow my learners to put their learning into a real context. In my 15 years of teaching, a common frustration amongst teachers is that pupils find it difficult to transfer the skills that they learn into different situations and, as a result, embed their learning securely. How many of us have taken on a class who claim to never have done dividing before? Or to have never seen speech marks before. We know they have; they just haven't retained it effectively.

Providing a context for learners to explore and play with concepts we teach them, will help them make sense of them in 'real life' and hopefully retain them for future use and recall it when required. Create an environment that invites questions, investigation and curiosity and allow your learners to access activities that meet their interests and specific needs. I have an Ideas Wall for my class to stick post-its with questions or suggestions. I endeavour to address all of them or allow time for the pupils to address them independently. If you have this ethos in your classroom, learners will independently seek to find out, explore and investigate, enhancing their learning styles but doing so using the play principles of free choice, intrinsic motivation, and personal drive. Children will learn from their own investigations, but they will also learn from their peers and their environment if they are given the opportunity to. Support your learners to reflect on their learning and progress in order to revisit it and build on it. I have seen a noticeable increase in pupils asking me if I have marked their work yet – they are keen to see how they have done, see if they have improved. Empower them to lead aspects of their own learning and they will engage and be motivated.

It is important to remember that the process is much more important than the product. Teaching children how to research a historical person that interests them, take notes, and turn their notes into something else, whether that's a poster, report, or presentation, is much more meaningful than the production of 30 reports on William Wallace. The first approach means the pupils will learn from each other and is much more interesting for you to assess as well!

Chapter 7: - Measuring Impact

Evidence is vital when you are introducing something new. There needs to be confirmation that what you are doing is worthwhile and having a positive impact on your learners. There is a variety of ways you can measure the impact of your play-based approach. You will have assessments that you would routinely do in your school that will show any increase in attainment and hopefully your new approach will be reflected in this. There are alternative measures you could take, such as engagement, involvement or application.

The Leuven 5-point Scale can be used to measure a learner's involvement in an activity.

THE LEUVEN SCALE FOR INVOLVEMENT

Level	Involvement	Signals
1	Extremely Low	Activity is simple, repetitive and passive. The child seems absent and displays no energy. They may stare into space or look around to see what others are doing.
2	Low	Frequently interrupted activity. The child will be engaged in the activity for some of the time they are observed, but there will be moments of non-activity when they will stare into space, or be distracted by what is going on around them.
3	Moderate	Mainly continuous activity. The child is bust with the activity but at a fairly routine level and there are few signs of real involvement. They make some progress with what they are doing but don't show much energy and concentration and can be easily distracted.
4	High	Continuous activity with intense moments. The child's activity has intense moments and at all times they seem involved. They are not easily distracted.
5	Extremely High	The child shows continuous and intense activity revealing the greatest involvement. They are concentrated, creative, energetic and persistent throughout nearly all the observed period.

It can be particularly useful for measuring engagement and involvement in play activities but focuses less on learning. In the Upper Stages, we may wish to measure not just engagement, but engagement in a specific, given task which is why I created my own scales of measurement.

In my Support for Learning role a few years ago, I worked closely with teachers and other colleagues, to create methods of measuring the impact of supportive interventions, including measuring engagement before

58

attempting to increase attainment. I wanted something that specifically measured engagement in learning Through this, I developed an Engagement Scale (see below), which I unashamedly and unoriginally named after myself and have used effectively to show changes in learner engagement in their learning. I have since developed this to be more in line with HMIe measures and now use to measure the engagement of targeted individuals in my class who have previously struggled to engage with their learning.

Following the use of my Engagement Scale, I then developed an Attainment Scale (see below), using similar HMIe-related levels to measure achieved attainment levels in any given lesson. While these are not yet widely recognised measurement scales, it doesn't hurt to have evidence behind you of any sort. If a specific measurement tool does not exist for what you are looking to measure, or you can't find a tool you need, sometimes you have to be innovative and create your own!

Simpson Engagement Scale

6	Listened to input, started activity & completed all/almost all (over 90%) of task independently – with or without stuck strategies.
5	Listened to input, completed most (75-90%) of task using agreed strategies independently.
4	Listened to input, started, and completed all/almost all of task (over 90%) with support to use agreed stuck strategies.
3	Listened to input, completed majority (50-74%) of task using agreed stuck strategies with support.
2	Listened to input, completed less than half (15-49%) of task.
1	In room but unable or unwilling to access support strategies. Less than 15% of task completed.
0	Disengaged from lesson, refusal to enter room or left room. Refusal to access support strategies. No work completed.

Simpson Attainment Scale

5	All or almost all task completed correctly. Over 90% of S.C. met
4	Most of task completed correctly. 75%-90% of S.C. met.
3	Majority of task completed correctly. 50%-74% of S.C. met.
2	Less than half of task completed correctly. 15%-49% of S.C. met.
1	Hardly any of task completed. Less than 15% of S.C. met.

Action Research

Measuring can be carried out in cycles either using an

APDR (Assess, Plan, Do, Review) or a PDSA (Plan, Do,

Study, Act). Examples of each of these can be found
below.

APDR – Assess, Plan, Do, Review

Assess Plan Do Review Recording Sheet

AIM What are our main questions/main aims and why? What are we trying to achieve?		Cycle No. & Start Date	Target group/issue	Review Date
Assess	What data do we have and what does it tell us? •			
	What else do we need to find out? •			
Plan	What is the intended outcome and how will we measure impact? How will we get this data? •			
	How do we plan to implement this change/intervention/address the identified need – who, what, why, where, when, how? •			
Do	What happened during implementation? -			
Review	What does the data tell us about the impact of this change/intervention? What does it tell us in relation to our aim?			
	What do we need to do next (ongoing assess, plan, do, review cycle)? -			
This template has been adapted from the PDSA template available on the Scottish Government website: www.gov.scot/Topics/Education/Schools/curriculum/Raisingeducationalattainment/RAFA/QIMaterial/programm etemplates				

PDSA – Plan, Do, Study, Act

Plan Do Study Act – Record of Activity

AIM Describe your first (or next) test of change: What are we trying to accomplish? Cycle number: 1		By whom?	When?	Where?
P	PLAN List the tasks needed to set up this test of change. How will we do it? •	By whom?	When?	Where?
	Predict what will happen when the test is carried out. What do you think will happen?	Measures to determine if prediction succeeds.		
D	DO Describe what happened when you ran the test •			
S	STUDY Describe the measured results and how they compared to the prediction. •			
A	ACT Describe what modifications to the plan will be made for the next cycle. •			

This template and headings have been taken from the Scottish Government website. Other content added by DEPS. www.gov.scot/Topics/Education/Schools/Raisingeducationalattainment/RAFA/QIMaterial

Both of these allow us to continuously reflect on our play pedagogy and adjust according to feedback from the learners. If they are not engaging with certain areas or resources, struggling to transition from play to more formal learning or not using the resources in the way you had hoped to extend their learning, change it. The APDR or PDSA allows you to have a record of what you have tried, what has worked and what has needed tweaked. It shows

62

you are continually reflecting on your practise and making changes accordingly.

Observations

Play in the early years is often measured through observations. Observations can be invaluable in recording how pupils engage in their play activities. In the upper stages, however, more emphasis is placed on attainment and formal assessments so while observations will be a good indicator of how learners engage with their activities, it might be more beneficial to also measure how this is transferring to other areas of their learning. One way to do this is to use something like the Skills Development Scotland Meta Skills Progression Framework (link in References Section) to record the development of skills. You can track the class as a whole - how are they accessing the areas? What are they doing? Who is working with who? Or you can make observations of areas and resources - How are the resources being used? What are they being used for? Are any being used more than others? Or you can select targeted learners, those who you are trying to engage more, support behaviour or raise attainment – observe their interactions, ask questions, and note their answers, listen to their conversations, monitor how they transfer their skills into other areas.

Pupil Feedback

One of the most valuable pieces of feedback for me has been from the pupils themselves. Hearing them be excited about their learning or say they are looking forward to coming in each morning makes my job a whole lot easier. There are pupils in my current class who previously recorded low engagement in their learning who now run in on a Monday morning to see what the new STEAM challenge is for the week. This kind of activity can also support attendance and late-coming if this is something you are targeting. As long as you have a way to record the pupils' responses and feedback to your approach, you have evidence.

Celebrate the Successes

We can record pupil feedback formally so that we have records, but I often ask pupils to share what they have been learning or send them to the Senior Management Team with a piece of their work created during a contextualised play activity. It helps reinforce to management that they are learning while they play but it also instils some pride in the pupils about their play. Their independent learning becomes more directed and purposeful as learners develop their skills and transfer what they have learned through our teaching as well as their own investigating. Have a class success book or share photos on a platform that your school are happy using and encourage your pupils to talk about their learning in a positive but educational way. "We played with the toy money today" doesn't sound as good as "we played shops where we had to stick to a budget, and I was only allowed to use my debit card for £30 of my shopping"!

Chapter 8: - Play in Practice – Real Examples

Creating Contextual Learning Opportunities

So, this is all well and good in theory. Contextual learning opportunities for all learners, continuous provision, incorporating pupil interest and ability and linking to learning where possible to develop skills and knowledge. Easy, right?!

Obviously not, otherwise we'd already all be doing it! Introducing the Principles of Play into an upper stages classroom is not something I can just tell you how to do. Disappointing, I know! But your class, your teaching style and your classroom are unique to you. What I can do, however, is tell you some of the methods of bringing these contextual opportunities into the classroom that have worked for me and some of my colleagues.

Something to remember is that, like everything else in our profession, there is no one size fits all approach. As a teacher, we need to find what will work for our learners and their specific needs. Whether you have a single stream or a composite class, 18 pupils or 33, few specific needs or many complex ones, we need to make sure we get it right for every child by tailoring our pedagogy to match our learners.

Classroom Set Up

Your classroom can be set up to have opportunities for Play available at all times. Continuous provision, as described in Chapter 1, should be freely available to learners and remain fairly constant throughout the year. Once it is set up, there shouldn't be much change required. This can be in the form of some trays or a couple of boxes on the windowsill or could be considered in our Numeracy and Literacy areas, which I imagine we all have in one form or another.

There are various ways we can do this in an older class. Depending on your classroom furniture and space, you can have shelves, windowsills or tables with baskets or boxes, or even use tray units to store play materials that learners can access independently. Label your trays clearly so all learners and visitors to the classroom know what is in each box or tray.

Have areas of the classroom that provide contextual opportunities without explicitly being for play. As learners grow and mature, their play changes. They can play with calculators, storyboards, puzzles or measuring tapes. I have had a cleaning station in my P6 classroom, complete with cloths, washing up liquid, spray bottles and a dustpan and brush as members of the class would regularly ask if they could clean the classroom. We even regularly borrow the cleaner's vacuum cleaner to 'play' at cleaning the classroom!

Resources

Apart from the interests of your learners, resourcing the play in your classroom will depend on a number of things: mainly available space, available funds and available support.

In an ideal world, we would all have space for different dedicated contextual areas, with money available for lots of new resources and at least one additional adult to help with observations and facilitating play with those who need support.

If space is limited, a tray unit can house all the different resources you need. If funding is tight, have a rummage through school cupboards. Most of my resources have been dug out of the back of colleagues' cupboards. I go with the theory that if it's covered in dust, it's up for grabs! If you have little or no support in the classroom, be creative with how you observe learning through play. Observe targeted pupils only, or occasionally ask pupils for feedback or to give peer feedback.

It is generally agreed that there are certain resources that are essential for play to meet developmental needs of our learners. While this tends to refer to those in the early years, they can certainly be adapted to be more appropriate for older learners.

Small World – traditionally a dolls' house with dolls for children to manipulate in whatever way helps them make sense of the world. In an upper stages classroom, this can be a box or tray with miniature characters and some furniture.

Home Corner – in the early years classroom, this might be a small kitchen area with various resources for playing house. For older learners this can be a box of items for them to use in a similar way – a phone, cups, plates, baby doll and saucepan have been enough for my class to create a whole story about family life.

Construction – this would look like large wooden blocks in a younger classroom, but in the upper stages it can be Lego, Kapla, K*Nex or any other materials the pupils can build creatively with. You can keep a box of this stuff under a table or on a windowsill or just in a tray in a tray unit. If you are so inclined, you can provide challenge cards or make themed activities for them. Or not, just providing the resources is enough.

Cars/Vehicles – a small box or tub of cars and other vehicles will do but if you have a bit more space, a roadmap or junk that could be used to create a landscape is great.

Art – Opportunities to be creative and artistic without teacher input are rare in the upper stages classroom. But it can be very tricky to find space for a designated art area. Even just storing your art resources somewhere that the pupils have access to can be enough. Allow them the option of choosing an arty activity when they are finished their non-negotiable task or at the end of the week. Perhaps use your judgement on the time needed to tidy up and which materials should be available. Pencils, crayons and paper all the time, paint and glitter only when you have the energy for them!

Reading/Writing Areas – most upper stages classrooms will have a library or reading area already. Why not add some paper and writing materials to the area to add an extra level of creativity? Different pens, blank jotters, and templates.

And mix up your reading materials if you can – books, comics, newspapers. Audio books and eBooks are a great alternative for reluctant readers if you have access to them. Give your learners some choice. Remember, it is not about giving yourself more to do, just giving the pupils more scope to be creative and play about with resources they already have. And opportunities to freely practice what we have been teaching them.

Maths/Numeracy – Again, you probably already have a Numeracy area, or at least a wall display. While an infant classroom might have a Tuff Tray with a range of materials for number activities, we can have a table of numeracy games, a tray of maths equipment (measuring tapes, timers, calculators etc.) or even a couple of poly pockets stuck to the wall with a fun challenge or games to try. Try to tailor your resources to whatever you are currently teaching. When teaching money, have some catalogues, play money and a till. When teaching measure, have some scales, tape measures and rulers in an accessible place.

Be creative, adapt resources you already have to make those that encourage a playful and contextual approach to learning. I have used the following ideas with some success and might be a good place to start:

Headbandz – create new cards with concepts you have been teaching

Guess Who – use in Literacy to develop descriptive language

Dice – for addition of 3, 4 or 5 numbers or multiplication up to 6 x 6. I have also created a bank of 6 topics, sentence starts, or challenges and the dice determine the task. Differently numbered dice can be used in place value, chance or probability activities.

Uno – for place value, creating 5-, 6-, 7-digit numbers and rearranging to create smaller numbers or discuss the impact of changing the digit in a specific place. There's a lot more that you can use these number cards for and I'm sure the children will come up with some!

Recording

As mentioned previously, there is a variety of ways you can record the impact of your Play/Contextual Opportunities. The ultimate measure of the impact of these contextual learning opportunities in an upper stages class are the attainment figures and feedback from your learners. Assessments and evidence of learning shows how the learners are progressing and comparisons with previous years' evidence the impact of the change in pedagogy. I do, however, have individual learners that I need to target to try and increase engagement and, hopefully, attainment. For these learners, I record engagement using my engagement scale and keep data specific to them. Feedback from the pupils is just as important. The class keep records of their learning through our Learning Journey – photos, quotes, recordings, and our Proud Book of achievements. Make sure to involve the pupils in the recording of progress and observations. It ensures they can talk confidently about their learning and the progress they are making. Their development as learners and as individuals is sometimes impossible to measure, but they are a living example of the difference you are making.

Logistics

Scheduling regular 'play' opportunities into your timetable might be next to impossible. It certainly has been for me. In my current P6 class, I put aside a session in the first week of term to discuss the meaning of play and contextualised learning for us and explained my target of raising their attainment alongside their desire to enjoy their learning. We agreed as a class how to set up the classroom and how to resource our Play Trays.

After the first week of term, we probably want to get into the serious learning more, so there needs to be a way to allow play and contextual learning to happen without negatively impacting attainment and the acquisition of skills.

If you can timetable opportunities and it works for your class, then that's great. What I have found more useful for my classes, is reassuring them that the play resources and opportunities are always available to them when they need them but not specifically timetabling sessions. Most of my learners like to access the contextual resources once they have completed their 'non-negotiable' task, if there is time, but some need to use the opportunities for breaks in their learning. As the term goes on, I find even my learners that struggle to engage in a full lesson will engage with the contextual learning resources as a means of taking a break. For me, this is an improvement on brain breaks that can see them removed from the classroom environment and their peers. It is worth mentioning though, that of course there are pupils who may need to have their break outside of the room or even outside of the school building, but in the main, keeping learners included with their own class is preferred.

I do schedule regular contextualised lessons, opportunities for pupils to apply their learning. This might take the form of some numeracy stations, a problem-solving challenge or a writing lesson focused on a real-life situation we are facing such as scripting our assembly or writing to local businesses for donations for a fundraiser.

While these opportunities are scheduled as necessary, I do timetable a regular slot on a Friday afternoon for us as a class, to reflect on our learning for the week and then learners choose an area to extend in any way they like. This year we have called it Independent Learning (pupil suggestion) and it essentially consists of us reviewing what we have learned that week, what we enjoyed, found challenging, and writing it into a big book. We then display the book, and everyone chooses something to extend for

45 minutes – the art lesson that they felt didn't go as well as they had hoped, writing their own book with a friend, playing shops, or even fixing corrections from their numeracy textbook (it has happened!). The session is without boundaries of task so pupils can take their learning in any direction they like. It is during these sessions that I have seen self-taught stop motion animation discovered, a volume of short stories created, and a small spa business set up. It's my favourite part of the week to observe how my learners apply their learning in different contexts and show their transference of skills.

Play is free flowing, and a context-driven approach requires a lot of flexibility from teachers. If a learner asks a question that is slightly off topic but nevertheless relevant, answer it. If the class show an interest when something out of the ordinary happens, dive right into it. If there is a fire drill and it sparks a discussion on the emergency services or what would we do if...? (every time!) then take 10 minutes or so to just go with it. Encourage their curiosity and inquisitiveness.

Typically, I start by thinking about my key subjects – Numeracy, Literacy and Health and Wellbeing. I still use textbooks, workbooks, and jotters, but I also have opportunities for the learners to choose how they want to extend their learning. Below, I have listed some areas of learning I have successfully found a balance for traditional teaching and assessment opportunities alongside pupil-led experiences and observations.

Numeracy and Maths

While I stand at the board and teach, encouraging discussion and explanation of strategies, there is an expectation that we will have some textbook work to complete that week. My class know, however, that once these tasks are completed, they will have some opportunities to apply their learning in a more active and contextualised way. When learning about money for example, once I have taught about decimals, finding totals, calculating change, sticking to a budget, I introduce some catalogues and money games to the numeracy table. Then we move on to learning about credit cards and debt, I provide plastic cards (although, by then a few pupils might have made their own anyway!), calculators and paper templates for keeping track of money in and out. If computer devices are available, I would also let them have time to explore spreadsheets or similar programmes.

Even when we are not explicitly learning about money, I will leave some play money out all year to allow revisiting and retrieval practice to take place. I will also, however, change the items on the Numeracy table depending on what we are learning about at the time and keep other items available in trays for the pupils to access independently whenever they need to.

Writing

I provide a slot (usually on Fridays, for the alliteration!) for Free Writing. We call it Free Write Fridays (I know!) and in that half hour pupils can write about anything they want (topic) in any style they want (story, newspaper article, comic strip) with anything they want (pen, pencil, crayon, laptop) and on anything they want (lined paper, giant paper, jotter, powerpoint, word). The results are always varied and very interesting, but it provides a stress-free writing experience for the learners that they know I will read and give feedback on, but not correct. I do use these pieces to inform my next steps in teaching though.

I also provide a range of writing materials on the Literacy table for learners to access when they need to, such as blank jotters, (half lined, half blank is great so they can illustrate their writing), blank comic strips, pens, coloured paper – whatever you can find in the cupboards! There's also some spelling and word games such as Scrabble and Sentence Scramble to allow opportunities for word practise.

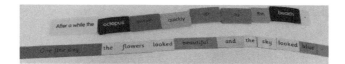

Reading

My reading corner has been designed and set up by my pupils. It is their reading area and I want them to have ownership of it. We start each term discussing the reading materials available to them. What books are they into? What authors to they want to include? What alternative materials do they want?

We usually have novels but also shorter stories and some picture books. I also have child-friendly newspapers, magazines, comics and, if I can, audio books. If the technology is available, I will also have eBooks on offer as well. Giving choice means allowing exploration and the hopeful discovery of something that interests them. The Guinness Book of Records is a must have in any upper stages class I have ever taught!

I feel a disclaimer is needed here: I am providing an account of my successes as I hope they will also be successful for others. Not every experience, however, has been successful! As alluded to, there have been situations where pupils struggle to move on from the play activities or refuse to complete the textbook work because they have enjoyed the play activity too much. There are still days where learners struggle to grasp a new concept or are reluctant to complete a task independently. This is not a cure for all struggles in the classroom. I have had a lot of trial and error when it comes to the materials and resources I provide for my class and their feedback has been vital. I try to tweak things in response to the learners, involve them in the development of our teaching and learning, give them ownership of their own progress. So, the moral of the story is that the best results come from working with your class, not for them. One of the joys of upper stages classes is the ability to get their ideas and feedback, planning with them, reflecting with them. Talk to them about what you hope this approach will achieve, how you want them to succeed and how this will look, namely with them attaining in the benchmarks for their level. In working together to try something new, the successes become something you work on as part of a team and can hopefully feel proud of as a team. Good luck!

I would love to see and hear about your experiences with a contextualised or play-based approach with the upper stages. Find me on Instagram @mrs_s_learns

References:

Broadhead, P., Howard, J., and Wood, E. (eds) (2010) Play and Learning in the Early Years: From Research to Practice. London: SAGE Publishing

Christie, J.F. and Roskos, K.A. (2006) Standards, Science and the Role of Play in Early Literacy Education. In Singer, D.G., Golinkoff, R.M., Hirsh-Pasek, K. (Eds) Play=Learning: How Play Motivates and Enhances Children's Cognitive and Social-Emotional Growth. Oxford University Press

Danniels, E. and Pyle, A. (2018) Defining Play-Based Learning http://ceril.net/index.php/articulos?id=594

Dearybury, J., & Jones, J. (2020) The Playful Classroom: The Power of Play for All Ages. Jossey-Bass: New Jersey

Fleer, M. (2021) Play in the Early Years (3rd Edition) Cambridge University Press

Gray, P. (2009) Play as a Foundation for Hunter-Gatherer Social Existence. American Journal of Play 1 pp476-522 in Fleer, M. (2021) Play in the Early Years (3rd Edition) Cambridge University Press

Krechevsky, M., Baldwin, M., Rodriguez, M.C., Christensen, L., Jorgensen, M., Jorgensen, O., Krishnadas, S., Overgaard, S., and Rabenhoj, T. (2019) Frankly It's a Gamble: What Happens When Middle

School Students Compose Their Own Schedules? *Scottish Educational Review* **51**(2) pp50-64

Lefa, B. (2014) The Piaget Theory of Cognitive Development: An Education Implication. *Educational Psychology* **1**(1) 9

McGuinness, c., Sproule, L., Bojke, C., Trew, K., & Walsh, g. (2014) *British Educational Research Journal*, **40**(5) (October 2014), pp. 772-795

McKendrick, J. (2019a) Shall the Twain Meet? Prospects for a Playfully Play-Full Scottish Education. *Scottish Educational Review* **51**(2) pp 3-13

McKendrick, J. (2019b) Realising the Potential of Play in Scottish Education. *Scottish Educational Review* **51**(2) pp137-142

Palmer, S. (2019) Why Scotland Needs a Kindergarten Stage (3-7 years), *Scottish Educational Review* **51**(2) pp87-95

Riley, J.G., and Jones, R.B. (2010) Acknowledging Learning Through Play in the Primary Grades. *Childhood Education* **86**(3) pp146-149

Scottish Executive (2004) *A Curriculum for Excellence.* Edinburgh: Scottish Executive

Scottish Executive (2007) Building the Curriculum 2
https://education.gov.scot/media/3mglewdo/btc2.pdf

Scottish Government (2008) Building the Curriculum 3
https://education.gov.scot/documents/btc3.pdf

Scottish Government, (2013) Play Strategy for Scotland:
Our Vision, Edinburgh: Scottish Government
https://www.gov.scot/publications/play-strategy-scotland-
vision/

Scottish Government, (2020a) United Nations Convention on
the Rights of the Child (Incorporation) (Scotland) Bill: leaflet
https://www.gov.scot/publications/united-nations-convention-
rights-child-incorporation-scotland-bill-
leaflet/#:~:text=The%20UNCRC%20%28Incorporation%29%20
%28Scotland%29%20Bill%20is%20a%20proposed,that%20ev
erything%20they%20do%20complies%20with%20children%20

Scottish Government (2021) Progress Review of
Scotland's Play Strategy 2021: Play in a Covid-19 Context
file:///C:/Users/abyss/OneDrive/Documents/Studying/MEd/
Innovation%20in%20Education/Play-Scotland-Play-
Strategy-Review-Play-in-Covid-2021.pdf

Sheridan, M.D. (2011) Play in Early Childhood: From Birth
to Six Years 3rd Edition Revised and Updated by Howard,
J. and Alderson, D. London: Routledge

Skills Development Scotland Meta Skills Framework –
https://www.skillsdevelopmentscotland.co.uk/media/48745
/meta-skills-progression-framework-final.pdf

UNICEF (2022) https://www.unicef.org/child-rights-
convention/convention-text-childrens-
version#:~:text=The%20United%20Nations%20Conventio
n%20on%20the%20Rights%20of,and%20they%20cannot
%20be%20taken%20away%20from%20children.

Walsh, G.M., McGuinness, C., Sproule, L., & Trew, K.
(2010) Implementing a play-based and developmentally
appropriate curriculum in Northern Ireland primary
schools: what lessons have we learned? *An International
Research Journal* **30**(1) pp53-66

Wood, E.A. (2013) Free Choice and Free Play in Early
Childhood Education: Troubling the Discourse.
International Journal of Early Years Education **22**(1) pp4-
18

Young, E. (2021) Let the Children Play: Research On The
Importance of Play, Digested. The British Psychological
Society 13th August 2021
https://digest.bps.org.uk/2021/08/13/let-the-children-play-
research-on-the-importance-of-play-digested/

Zachariou, A. and Whitebread, D. (2015) Musical Play and
Self-Regulation: Does Musical Play Allow for the
Emergence of Self-Regulatory Behaviours? *International
Journal of Play* **5**(1), pp116-135